Dobro Case
Chord Book

By Stacy Phillips

Copyright © 1988 by Amsco Publications,
A Division of Music Sales Corporation, New York, NY.

Order No. AM 67158
US International Standard Book Number: 978.0.8256.1124.7
UK International Standard Book Number: 0.7119.1243.2

Art direction by Mike Bell (UK)
Cover designed by Peter Hodkinson (UK)
Cover photography by Jonathan Pickow (US)
Interior photos by Georgia Sheron

EXCLUSIVELY DISTRIBUTED BY

HAL•LEONARD®

Contents

Introduction   5

Tablature Notation   7

Chord Recipes   9

How to Use This Book   12

The Chords
  C Major Triads   15
  C Major Seventh Chords
  (and Embellishments)   15
  Other C Major Chords   18
  D Minor Triads   19
  Other D Minor Chords   19
  Selected E Minor Chords   21
  Selected F Major Chords   22
  Other F Major Chords   22
  G Dominant Seventh Chords   23
  Other G Dominant Seventh Chords   24
  Selected A Minor Chords   26
  B Half-Diminished Seventh Chords   27
  C Diminished Chords   27

Technical Considerations   28
  Assorted Chords with Open Strings   30

Comping to Standard Progressions   32
  Rhythm Changes   33
  Jersey Bounce   36
  You've Changed   37

Some Useful Mini Chord Progressions   39

Introduction

The Hawaiian steel guitar is at some disadvantage when it comes to playing chords that are altered from the basic major triads. Fretting with a rod of metal is like playing with one finger—so how do you play the many crooked chords that seem to require an angular bar?

The first approach to solving this problem was made in the 1930s. This method involved changing the original open-chord tunings to ones containing various members of the diatonic scale. Then came added strings and necks, and, more recently, pedals to change a string's pitch without moving the bar. However, the six-string Dobro, tuned to an open G, has remained the instrument of choice in the country, bluegrass, and folk music fields. Now a new generation of Dobroists are expanding their chosen instrument's repertoire. This again raises the question of how to handle embellished chords. The *Dobro Case Chord Book* addresses this problem.

G tuning does limit the number of complete chords that can be played on a Dobro. However, all the notes of a chord are not needed to define its sound. Most of the chord positions in this book use three notes. If you are playing with another instrumentalist, three-note chords are fully sufficient for creating interesting harmonic statements. While the Dobro's role may never be that of a primary rhythm instrument, it is well-suited to punctuating rhythms and providing thickness to the harmonic backdrop of a song. This function is sometimes called *comping* (from accompaniment). Comping involves the insertion of one or two strums per measure, in contrast to the more constant flow of a drum or bass. These strums can be syncopated or on the beat, simple major triads, or highly substituted flat-five or sharp-eleven chords—it all depends on the kind of music you are playing and the mood you wish to set.

The following list of chord positions provides the instrumentalist with comping ideas. The use of the Dobro as a rhythmic and harmonic instrument has never been fully explored, and this book is designed to stimulate interest in these areas. Equally useful is the way the following chord forms can be applied to lead work, allowing for a mix of both single note and chordal approaches in your solos. Of course, you can also play these positions as arpeggios in single-string lines.

Tablature Notation

Each line of tablature represents a string in standard tuning, with the lowest (G) at the bottom and the highest (D) at the top.

```
First String  ─D─────────────────
Second String ─B─────────────────
Third String  ─G─────────────────
Fourth String ─D─────────────────
Fifth String  ─B─────────────────
Sixth String  ─G─────────────────
```

The numbers refer to the frets to be barred. Thus, the next example indicates that you play the first string at the ninth fret, the third string at the eighth fret, and the fifth string at the seventh fret, all at the same time.

```
T───────9──────────────────────
A───────8──────────────────────
B───────7──────────────────────
```

Here are some markings that appear specifically in Dobro notation.

↑   An arrow placed to the right of a note means that you should pull the indicated string behind the bar so that its pitch is raised one fret. So, 5↑ means that, even though the bar is on the fifth fret, the string should sound as if it was barred on the sixth fret.

↑↑ Two arrows placed to the right of a note means that you should pull the pitch of the string up two frets. So, 5↑↑ means that the bar is on the fifth fret, but the string sounds the pitch of the seventh fret.

*   An asterisk to the right of a note means that you should bend the string up to the pitch of the indicated fret. This symbol only occurs in slant positions. In the following example, when the first and third strings are in tune, the second is barred between the fourth and fifth frets. So, you should pull the string until it sounds the pitch of the fifth fret.

```
T───────5──────────────────────
        5*
A───────4──────────────────────
B──────────────────────────────
```

Similarly, 5*↑ means to pull the pitch about a fret-and-a-half up (to the sixth fret). Consult my *Dobro Book* for a discussion of pulled string technique.

Chord Recipes

To help you cope with the welter of chords that follow, here is a short guide to their identification and manufacture. There is no need to memorize any of this before continuing. You can learn by using the chords, and use this section as a reference.

Chord names are based on the major scale and are numbered, starting with the key or tonic note. This is the C major scale.

scale note:	C	D	E	F	G	A	B	C	D	E	F	G	A
step number:	1	2	3	4	5	6	7	8	9	10	11	12	13

There are two frets (or one *whole step*) between some of the notes and one fret (or one *half step*) between others.

scale note: C	D	E	F	G	A	B	C
interval:	whole step	whole step	half step	whole step	whole step	whole step	half step

The standard Western major scale always has this same order of intervals between notes.

The naturally occurring chords of this *diatonic scale* are assembled by piling alternate notes on each scale step. For example, the chord at the first step contains the first, third, and fifth notes of the scale (C, E, and G—a major triad). Note that there are two whole steps (four frets) between the first and third notes and one-and-one-half steps (three frets) between the third and fifth notes. This is the recipe for all major triads.

Adding additional alternate steps creates *embellished chords*. For example, C, E, G, and B make up a *C major seventh chord* (notated CΔ7). C, E, G, B, and D make up a *C major ninth chord* (notated CΔ9).

The diagram below depicts four-note chords built on each step of the scale to form the naturally occurring seventh chords in the key of C.

	B	C	D	E	F	G	A
	G	A	B	C	D	E	F
	E	F	G	A	B	C	D
	C	D	E	F	G	A	B
chord name:	CΔ7	Dm7	Em7	FΔ7	G7	Am7	Bm7♭5
chord number:	IΔ7	IIm7	IIIm7	IVΔ7	V7	VIm7	VIIm7♭5

You can safely solo over any of these chords with a C major scale. The IΔ7 and IVΔ7 chords (those built on the first and fourth scale steps) are *major seventh chords*. The IIm7, IIIm7, and VIm7 chords are *minor seventh chords*. Compare the number of steps between the notes of the major and minor seventh chords. The third and seventh scale steps of the latter chords are flatted by one fret. The note one fret down from the major seventh step is simply called the seventh. Thus, using Dm7 as an example, the formula for forming a minor seventh chord is as follows.

scale note: D		F		A		C
interval:	whole step	half step	whole step	whole step	whole step	half step

The chord built on the seventh step is a minor seventh with its fifth note flatted by one fret. This chord is also called a *B half-diminished seventh chord* (notated B⌀7).

A *flat sign* (♭) before a scale step number means to flat that note by one fret. A *sharp sign* (♯) means to raise the note one fret. Note that scale notes are

CHORD TYPE	CHORD SYMBOL
major seventh	CΔ7
major ninth	CΔ9
major eleventh	CΔ11
major seventh (add sixth)	CΔ7(add 6)
major sixth	C6
six-nine	C 6/9
major suspended fourth	Csus4
major flatted fifth	C(♭5)
major ninth flatted fifth	CΔ9(♭5)
augmented	C +
minor seventh	Dm7
minor ninth	Dm9
minor (major seventh)	Dm(Δ7)
minor sixth	Dm6
minor sixth (add ninth)	Dm6(add 9)
seventh	G7
ninth	G9
eleventh	G11
thirteenth	G13
seventh flatted fifth	G7♭5
augmented seventh	G7 +
seventh suspended fourth	G7sus4
seventh sharped ninth	G7♯9
seventh flatted ninth	G7♭9
seventh flatted fifth sharped ninth	G7♯5♭9
half-diminished seventh (minor seventh flatted fifth)	B⌀7

One other important chord type is formed by playing notes separated by three frets. Here is the chromatic scale with these notes circled.

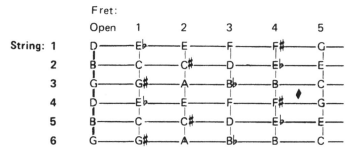

marked with Arabic numerals, while chords are notated with Roman numerals.

The chart below contains some common chords with the various additions and substitutions that are integral to Western popular and jazz music. Note that every note of each chord need not be played to express its essence.

SCALE STEPS	NOTES
1, 3, 5, 7	C, E, G, B
1, 3, 5, 7, 9	C, E, G, B, D
1, 3, 5, 7, 9, 11	C, E, G, B, D, F
1, 3, 5, 6, 7	C, E, G, A, B
1, 3, 5, 6	C, E, G, A
1, 3, 5, 6, 9	C, E, G, A, D
1, 3, 4, 5	C, E, F, G
1, 3, $\flat$5	C, E, G$\flat$
1, 3, $\flat$5, 7, 9	C, E, G$\flat$, B, D
1, 3, $\sharp$5	C, E, G$\sharp$
1, $\flat$3, 5, $\flat$7	D, F, A, C
1, $\flat$3, 5, $\flat$7, 9	D, F, A, C, E
1, $\flat$3, 5, 7	D, F, A, C$\sharp$
1, $\flat$3, 5, 6	D, F, A, B
1, $\flat$3, 5, 6, 9	D, F, A, B, E
1, 3, 5, $\flat$7	G, B, D, F
1, 3, 5, $\flat$7, 9	G, B, D, F, A
1, 3, 5, $\flat$7, 9, 11	G, B, D, F, A, C
1, 3, 5, $\flat$7, (9), (11), 13	G, B, D, F, (A), (C), E
1, 3, $\flat$5, $\flat$7	G, B, D$\flat$, F
1, 3, $\sharp$5, $\flat$7	G, B, D$\sharp$, F
1, 3, 4, 5, $\flat$7	G, B, C, D, F
1, 3, 5, $\flat$7, $\sharp$9	G, B, D, F, A$\sharp$
1, 3, $\flat$5, $\flat$7, $\flat$9	G, B, D, F, A$\flat$
1, 3, $\flat$5, $\flat$7, $\sharp$9	G, B, D$\flat$, F, A$\sharp$
1, $\flat$3, $\flat$5, $\flat$7	B, D, F, A

This is called a *diminished chord.* After four notes, the formula repeats. Thus, there are only three unique diminished chords: C°, C$\sharp$°, and D°. Here are those chords and their equivalents.

$$C° = D\sharp° = F\sharp° = A°$$
$$C\sharp = E° = G° = A\sharp°$$
$$D° = F° = G\sharp° = B°$$

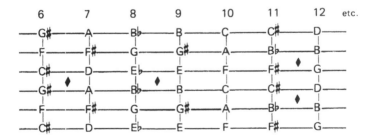

How to Use This Book

The diagrams that follow provide the Dobro player with different approaches to playing the chord types just discussed. This listing is by no means exhaustive. If you have the inclination, you may discover additional positions for these chords and new forms for chords which are not included.

The key of C provides the framework for the diagrams that follow. Within each section, the chord types are arranged in order of increasing harmonic content and tension. If you wish to play a chord in a different key, simply shift the given position up or down the appropriate number of frets.

Here is an example. If you want a G♭m6, you can look under Dm6 (or Em6 or Am6) and perhaps choose this form.

Dm6

```
 T ──────15──────────────────────
 A ──────15↑─────────────────────
 B ──────15──────────────────────
   ──────────────────────────────
```

Since G♭ is four frets higher than D, the equivalent position is as follows.

G♭m6

```
 T ──────19──────────────────────
 A ──────19↑─────────────────────
 B ──────19──────────────────────
   ──────────────────────────────
```

Here it is an octave lower.

G♭m6

```
 T ───────7──────────────────────
 A ───────7↑─────────────────────
 B ───────7──────────────────────
   ──────────────────────────────
```

Here is another example. If you want a C7♯9 chord, look up the G7♯9 forms. You might choose this chord form.

G7♯9

```
 T ──────11──────────────────────
 A ──────10──────────────────────
 B ───────9──────────────────────
   ──────────────────────────────
```

To form a C7♯9 chord, transpose this up five frets.

C7♯9

```
 T ──────16──────────────────────
 A ──────15──────────────────────
 B ──────14──────────────────────
   ──────────────────────────────
```

Or, you could transpose it down seven frets, to the same end.

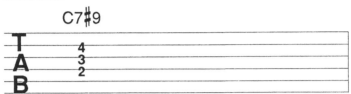

The naturally occurring chords of the first and fourth steps of the diatonic major scale are both major. For this reason, after all the C major positions, only selected samples of F major chords are listed to provide additional examples of shifting a bar position from one chord to another. The same format is followed with the three-note minor chords.

Some voicings and inversions may work better in certain keys, or sound better shifted up or down an octave. Experimentation is the way to find out which voicings are most effective.

After all the chord diagrams, some practical uses of the forms are presented. A few common chord progressions from the field of pop music standards are used as matrices to show how these bar positions work in practice. Here you will see why the obvious bar position is not necessarily the best. Here's an example of a subsitute chord form that might be handier than the more obvious form.

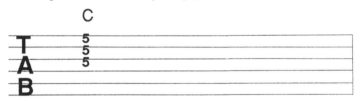

This equivalent form may simply not be as effective.

C

```
T---------5-------
A---------5-------
---------5-------
B----------------
```

The section that follows provides some short chord progressions that may also be used as parts of solos.

The Chords

C Major Triads

C

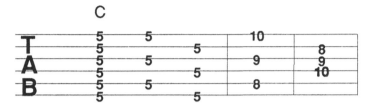

C Major Seventh Chords (and Embellishments)

CΔ7

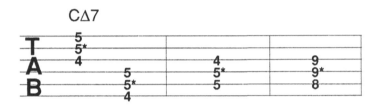

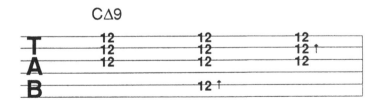

CΔ9

CΔ11

CΔ7(add6)

C6

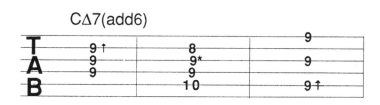

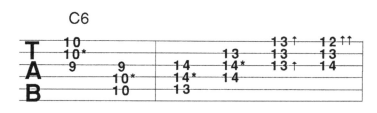

```
T|--8↑↑----|--7-----7----|--14---------|
 |--9------|--8-----8----|-------13----|
A|--10-----|--9-----9----|--14*--------|
 |---------|--------10---|-------14*---|
B|---------|-------------|--13---------|
 |---------|-------------|-------14----|
```

```
T|--10-----|-------------|--5↑↑----|--8↑↑----|
 |--10*----|--10---------|---------|---------|
A|--9------|--10*--------|--5------|--9------|
 |---------|-------------|---------|--10-----|
B|--8------|-------------|--5------|---------|
 |---------|--9----------|---------|---------|
```

C6/9

```
T|--7↑----14↑--|--15---------|--12---------|--7↑----14↑--|
 |--7-----14---|--16*--------|--13---------|-------------|
A|--7-----14---|-------------|--14---------|--7-----14---|
 |-------------|--17---------|-------------|-------------|
B|-------------|-------------|-------------|--7-----14---|
 |-------------|-------------|-------------|-------------|
```

Csus4

```
T|--5↑----|--5↑---------|-------------|-------------|
 |--5-----|-------------|--10---------|--10---------|
A|--5-----|--5----------|--10*--------|--10---------|
 |--------|-------------|-------------|--8----------|
B|--------|--5----------|--9----------|-------------|
 |--------|-------------|-------------|-------------|
```

Other C Major Chords

C(♭5)

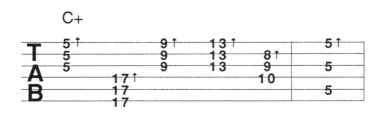

CΔ9(♭5)

C+

D Minor Triads

Dm

```
T ──────6↑────5↑↑──15──────────────────
  ─6─────6─────6───15*──────────13↑↑────
A ─7*──7─6↑────7───14────14─────14──────
  ─7──7*──────────────────15*───15──────
B ─6───────────────15───────────────────
  ──────────────────15──────────────────
```

```
T ──────7──────────────10↑↑──13↑↑───────
  ───────────6────15────────────────────
A ──────7*──────────────10────14─────────
  ────────────7*────15*──────────────────
B ─6────────────────────10────15─────────
  ──────────7─────14─────────────────────
```

Other D Minor Chords

Dm7

```
T ──────10────7──────────15──────────────
  ──────10────6────13────15*───13─────────
A ──────10────5────14────14────14─────────
  ──────10──────────15──────────15*────────
B ──────10───────────────13────15─────────
  ──────10──────────────────────────────
```

```
T ──────10─────────────────────15─────────
  ────────────────10────────────────────
A ──────10─────────────────────14─────────
  ─────────────────10──────────────────
B ──────10─────────────────────13─────────
  ─────────────────10──────────────────
```

Dm9

```
T ──────10─────────────────────────────
  ──────10*──────────────────────13──────
A ──────9─────9──────9────14────14*──────
  ──────────10*────10*──14*────14─────────
B ──────────10──────────13──────────────
  ──────────────10──────────────────────
```

```
T ──────────────13↑──────────────14──────
  ──────14↑────13─────10──────────────────
A ──────14─────13↑────────────────14*──────
  ──────14──────────10*──────────────────
B ────────────────────────────────13──────
  ──────────────────9────────────────────
```

Dm7sus4

```
T--7↑--------5↑----|--7↑--------5↑--
A--7---------5-----|--7---------5---
B--7---------5-----|----------------
                   |--7---------5---
```

Dm(Δ7)

```
T----6↑------10↑----14↑-------------------
A----6-------10-----14-----14------13↑-----
-----6-------10-----14-----14------14------
B----------------------------14↑----15-----
```

```
T----6↑-----------10↑----------14↑--------
A----6------------10------------14---------
B----6------------10------------14---------
```

Dm6

```
T----15----------9----|----9-------15-----
-----15----10----10*--|--------------------
A----15↑---10*---10---|----10*-----15↑-----
-----15----9----------|--------------------
B----15---------------|----10------15------
```

Dm6(add9)

```
T----5----------9↑----|----9↑----
A----4----------9-----|----9-----
-----3----------9-----|----9-----
B---------------------|----9-----
```

Selected E Minor Chords

(see D Minor Chords for other forms)

Em

```
         7↑↑   5            12↑↑
T        8     5*      8           5
A    9   9     4       9*          5*
    9*                       12
B   8                        12
                 9           12    4
```

Em7

```
            9                    5
T           8          3
            7          4         4
A   12                 5
    12                           3
B   12
```

Em9

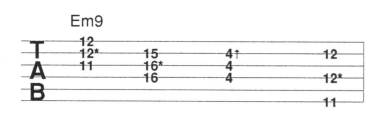

```
    12
T   12*    15      4↑          12
    11     16*     4
           16      4           12*
B
                               11
```

Em7sus4   Em(Δ7)

```
                          12↑   4↑   8↑
T    9↑    7↑             12    4    8
     9                    12    4    8
A    9     7
B          7
```

Em6

```
    8↑     16↑         5              17
T                      5↑      12
A   8      16          5       12*    17↑
                               11
B   8      16                         17
```

Em6(add9)

```
    7          11↑          11↑
T   6          11
A   5          11           11
B                           11
```

Selected F Major Chords

(see C Major Chords for other forms)

F

```
   10                    3
T  10           13
A  10           14       2
   10           15
B  10                    1
   10
```

FΔ7

```
   10        13↑   14          5↑↑
T  10*       13           10
A  9    14   13    14*         5
        14*              10*
B       13         13          5
                         9
```

FΔ9

```
   5     5          14   7    5
T  5     5↑   8     13   8         5↑
A  5     5    9     12   9    5
                10                5
B                       5
                                  5
```

FΔ11   **FΔ7(add6)**

```
   8↑            11      14↑        14
T  8      15             14         14
A  8      14     10      14
B         13                        14↑
               9
```

Other F Major Chords

F6

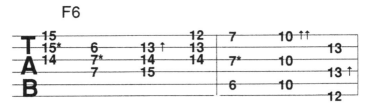

F6/9   Fsus4

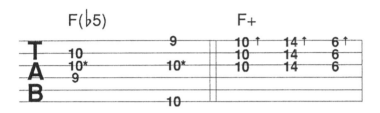

F(♭5)   F+

G Dominant Seventh Chords

G7

Other G Dominant Seventh Chords

G9

```
T --15---------------------|-----------------------|--18↑------17↑↑--
  --15*--------------------|--10---------10--------|--18-------18----
A --14---------14----------|--10*--------10*-------|--18↑------19----
  -------------15*---------|--9----------9---------|-----------------
B ------------15-----------|--8--------------------|-----------------
```

```
T -----------9------------|-------------------------|----------------
  -----------10*----------|--13↑↑-------------------|--6---------6---
A --7--------10-----------|--14---------------------|--7*--------7*--
  --7*--------------------|--15---------------------|--7---------7---
B --6---------------------|-------------------------|--8---------8---
```

```
T --------7-------10↑↑------13↑↑-------9--------
  --15----------------------------------------
A --15*---7*------10--------14--------10*------
  --------6-------10--------15--------10-------
B --14----------------------------------------
```

G11

```
T --10-----------|--15--------|--10-----------
  --10-----------|--15*-------|----------10---
A --10-----------|--14--------|--10-----------
  --10-----------|------------|----------10---
B --10-----------|--13--------|--10-----------
  --10-----------|------------|----------10---
```

G13   ### G7♭5

```
T --------17--------------15-------|---------5----
  --5-----17------15↑↑-----------|--6-------6*--
A --4-----16------16------16------|--5*------6---
  --3-----15------17--------------|--5-----------
B ----------------18------17------|--------------
```

```
T --------11--------------11-------|---------------
  --------11*↑-------------------|----------6----
A --4-----10------10------10*-----|--6*------6*--
  --3-------------11------9-------|--5-------5---
B --2-------------12--------------|--------------
  --------------------------------|--4-------4---
```

G9♭5

G7+   G7sus4

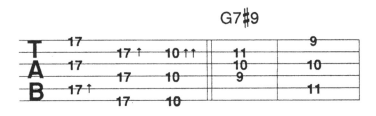

G7♯9

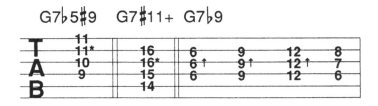

G7♭5♯9   G7♯11+   G7♭9

Selected A Minor Chords
(see D Minor Chords for other forms)

Am

```
T|------------13↑--------------------------|---14------8↑↑-|
A|----13------13----------------8↑↑--------|---13----------|
 |----14*-----13↑-----9--------9-----------|---14*-----9---|
 |----14--------------10*------10----------|---------------|
B|------------------10---------------------|---13------10--|
```

Am7

```
T|-----5------------10--------------10-----|
A|-----5------------10*--------------------|
 |-----5------------9---------------9------|
 |-----------------------------------------|
B|----------------8---------------8--------|
```

Am9   ### Am7sus4

```
T|---------------------9--------|||---12↑-----14↑-|
A|--------9↑-----------9*-------|||---12----------|
 |---4------9------9--------9---|||---12------14--|
 |---5*-----9*-----9-----------|||---------------|
B|---5------8------8-----------8|||-----------14--|
```

Am(△7)

```
T|----13↑----9↑---------------5↑-----9↑----|
A|----13-----9------8↑--------------------|
 |----13-----9------9--------5------9------|
 |------------------10---------------------|
B|--------------------------5------9------|
```

Am6   ### Am6(add9)

```
T|-----------------10------4-------|||-----------------16-|
A|----10-----5--------------------|||---12-----16↑-------|
 |----10↑----5*-----10↑-----5*----|||---11-----------16--|
 |----10-----4--------------------|||---10-----16--------|
B|----------------10------5-------|||-----------------16↑|
                                   |||---------------16--|
```

B Half-Diminished Seventh Chords

B⌀7

```
T--15-----15-----------------------|--------------------|
T--15*----15-----------14↑----------|--6-----------------|
A--14-----15↑----14----14-----------|--7*----7-----------|
A--------15-----15*---14↑----------|--7-----7*----------|
B--------15-----15-----------------|--------6-----------|
```

```
T----6↑-------------15---------------------7-----------|
T----6------10--------------15----15------------------|
A----6↑-----10*-----15↑---------------------7*---------|
A-----------9--------------15-----15*------------------|
B-------------------15------------------------6--------|
B-------------------------15↑----14--------------------|
```

C Diminished Chords

C°7

```
T----4------------------13----4------|
T----4------7----10------------------|
A----4↑-----7↑---10↑----13↑---13↑---4↑|
A-----------7----10-----13-----------|
B-----------------------13----13----4|
```

Technical Considerations

For many of you, reverse slants and string pulls may be novel techniques. Be aware not to overtax your pulling finger. If you want to pursue string bending in a big way, consider using relatively light gauge strings to reduce the strain.

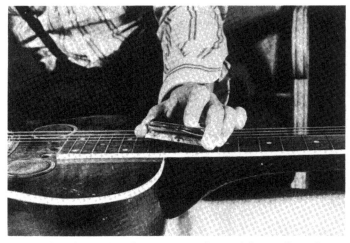

Proper hand position for a reverse slant with a pull on the first string

Usually, the barring hand is available to do any damping that is necessary. However, when moving between two positions while string pulling, the usual blocking fingers will be busy pulling, so you might consider damping with your picking hand instead.

There are a couple of bar positions where, as a last resort, you might need to fudge being in tune by using vibrato to befog the issue. A prime candidate for this procedure might be this position:

```
T----------17----------------------------
---------17----------------------------
A---------16----------------------------
---------15----------------------------
B----------------------------------------
```

Another trick for altering the pitch of a note without moving the bar is to actually depress the string to the neck. I have seen this done by bottleneck guitarists with relatively low string action. A Dobro's high action makes this very tricky to get in tune for several reasons.

- If you use very heavy strings, you may not want to exert extra pressure on the resonator. Your particular set-up may help you circumvent this problem.

- Considerable muscle may be needed to push the string all the way to the neck. Again, this is largely a function of string gauge.

- The string will not hit the frets (because of the extreme angle), so to sound a note one fret lower than the bar position, you might have to finger the string more than one fret lower. For example, you might want to get this chord.

28

```
T ----------12----------------------------
----------11----------------------------
A ----------12----------------------------
B ----------------------------------------
```

But, to do so, you may have to touch the second string to the fingerboard about one-and-a-half frets behind the bar.

Solving problems like these will provide you with some exciting possibilities.

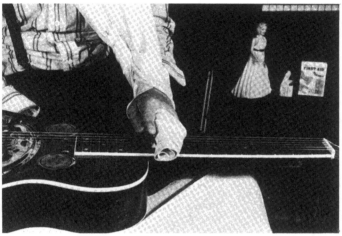

Do not overtax your pulling finger.

Assorted Chords with
Open Strings

CΔ7 CΔ9 Cm

```
T ---0----|---0----|--------
A ---0----|---0----|---0----
  ---5----|---5----|---1----
B ---5----|---5----|---1----
  ---5----|---5----|--------
```

Db7 Dm D6

```
T ----------||---3-----0---||---0----
A ---0------||---------10---||---0----
  ---6------||---2-----10---||---7----
  ---6------||---0---------||---7----
B ---6------||-------------||---7----
  ---6------||-------------||---7----
```

EbΔ7 Eb7+ Em

```
T ---0-----||--------------||---2----------
A ---8-----||---0-----0----||---0-----0----
  ---------||---0-----0----||---0-----0----
  ---8-----||---11---------||----------2---
B ---------||---------2----||--------------
```

Em7 Em6 E7

```
T ---0-----||--------------||---0----
A ---0-----||---0----------||---9----
  ---0-----||---0----------||---9----
  ---2-----||---2----------||---9----
B ---------||---2----------||---9----
                            ---9----
```

F6 Fm6

```
T ---0-----||---0---------0----
A ---10----||---6---------9----
  ---10----||------------------
  ---10----||---6--------10----
B ---10----||------------------
  ---10----||------------------
```

G7 Gm

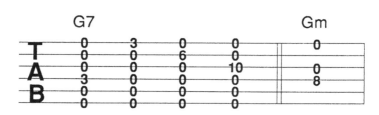

```
T ---0----3----0----0-----||---0----
A ---0----0----6----0-----||--------
  ---0----0----0---10-----||---0----
  ---3----0----0----0-----||---8----
B ---0----0----0----0-----||--------
  ---0----0----0----0-----||--------
```

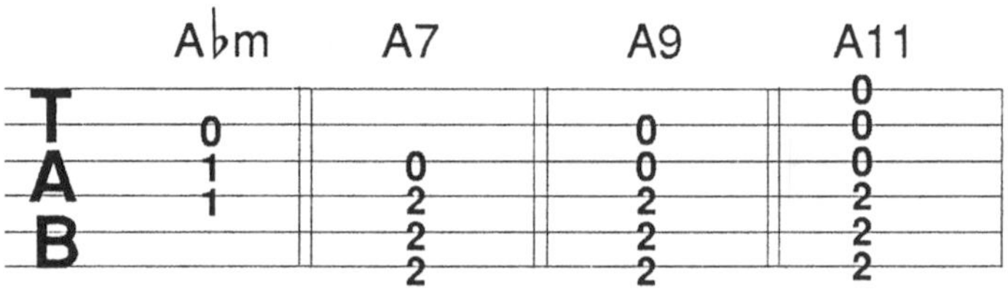
A♭m
A7
A9
A11
TAB

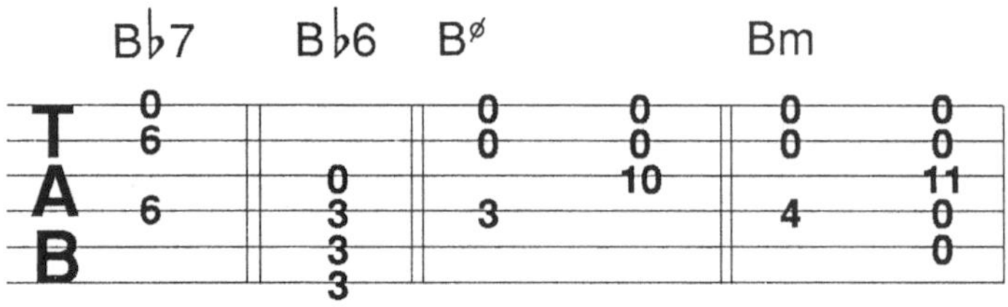
B♭7
B♭6
Bø
Bm
TAB

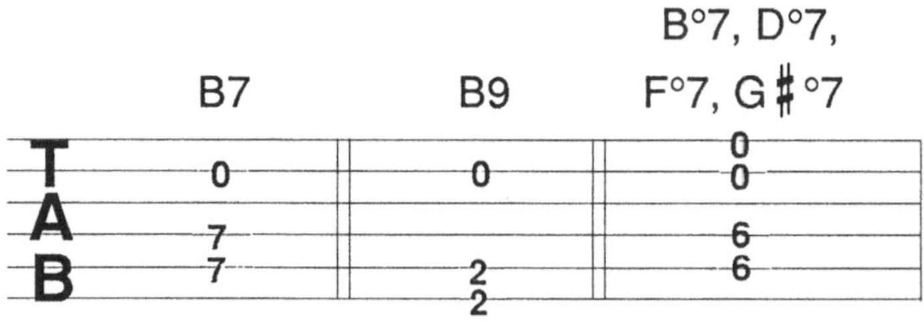
B7
B9
B°7, D°7,
F°7, G♯°7
TAB

Comping to Standard Progressions

This first progression is based on George Gershwin's "I Got Rhythm." It has been used in many other jazz tunes: "You'se a Viper" by Howard, Malcolm, and Moren; "Cottontail" by Duke Ellington; "Oreo" by Sonny Rollins; "Dexterity" by Charlie Parker; and "Angel Voice" by Ornette Coleman; to name a few. This standard jazz pattern is simply referred to as *rhythm changes*. You may find that the arrangement is a little busy, but this is because it is meant to illustrate the placement of many chord forms. If the tune is played at a fast tempo, it is probably best to leave out some of the chords—perhaps every other one in the first section.

When comping, it is a good idea to keep one or two notes sounding constantly throughout a few chords. It cuts down on bar movement and, most importantly, it is pleasing to the ear.

It is assumed that you are accompanied by at least a bass line to establish the root notes of the progression. When there are two chords in a measure, each occupies two beats. The first part (the *A section*) is played twice. Then play one *B section,* followed by one more A section, and ending on a B♭ chord.

¢	B♭ Gm7	Cm7 F7	B♭ Gm7	Cm7 F7
B♭△ B♭7	E♭ E♭m7	B♭ F7	B♭	*Fine* :‖
D7	D7	G7	G7	C7	C7	F7	F7 ‖

D.C. al Fine

Here are some comping chords that emphasize this harmonic foundation.

Rhythm Changes

	Bb	Gm7	Cm	F9
T			1	1
		3	1	1
A		3	0	0
		3 3		
B				

	Bb6	Gm	Cm7	Fsus4	Bb6	Bb7
T	8	8	8		8	8
	8*	8*	8	10 ↑	8*	8* ↑
A	7	7	8	10	7	7
			8	10		
B						

	Eb	Ebm7	Bb	F7b5		Bb6
T	8					
	8	11				
A	8	11	15	14		12
		11	15	13		12*
B			15	12		11

	Bb	Gm	Cm	F7b5	Bb	Gm6
T					15	15
	15	12	12	14	15	15*
A	15	12*	13*	13	15	14
	15	11	13	12		
B						

	Cm6	F7+	Bb	Bb7	Eb	Ebm
T	13	14			8	7
	13 ↑	13*	15	13	8	8*
A	13	13	15	12	8	8
			15	11		
B						

Bb   F11   Bb△7   D7

```
T--6----8-----------10----10----
A--7----8----7------10†---10†---
   8----8----7*-----10----10----
B------------6-------------------
```

G9   C13

```
T--10----10----10----10----
A--10*---10*----9-----9-----
    9-----9-----8-----8-----
B---------------------------
```

F7#9   Bb   Gm7   C7   F9

```
T---------------8-----3-----5-----5----
A--9----9-------7-----3-----4*----4*---
   8----8------------------------------
   7----7------------------------------
B---------------6-----3-----3-----3----
```

Bb   Gm   Cm   F7   Bb   Bb7

```
T-------12----8††---13----8----------
   15-------------------------------7--
A--15---12*---8-----13†---7----------
B-------11----8-----13----6---------6--
   15--------------------------------5--
```

Eb   Ebm6   Bb   F7   Bb

```
T-------4-----3------------------
   8--------------4--------3------
A-------4†----3-----------------
   8---------------3-------3------
B------4-----3-------------------
   8--------------2--------3------
```

"Jersey Bounce" is a medium tempo swing standard. Here are the chords. After you finish the B section, repeat the A section, with the second ending.

| ¢ | C | C | D7 | D7 | G7 | G7 | **1.** C C° | Dm G7 :|| |

| **2.** C A♭7 | C ‖ C7 | C7 | B♭7 | A♭7 | A♭7 | G7 | G7 ‖ |

Fine   *D.C. al Fine*

In the first section of this arrangement, there is some added harmonic motion. In the second measure, the diagonal lines represent the number of beats per chord position. As in the rhythm changes, here, the actual function of each shape is noted over the tablature lines.

Jersey Bounce

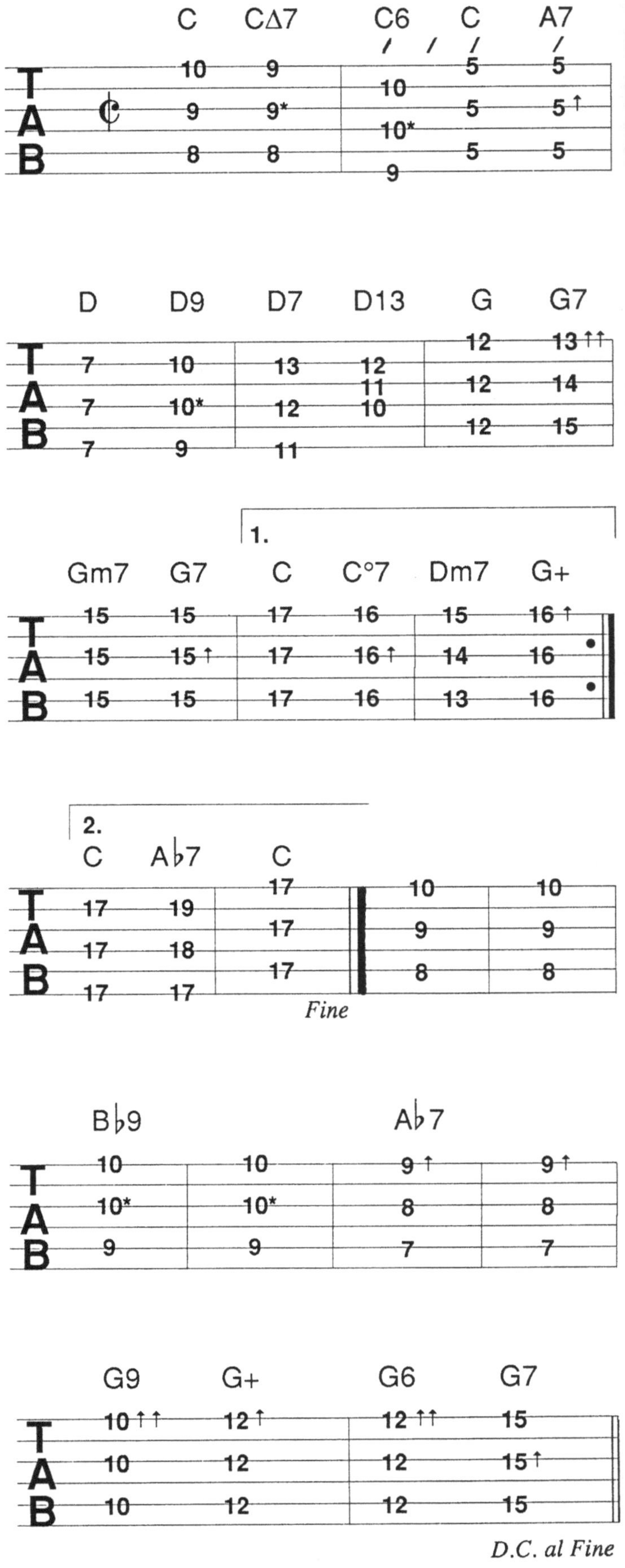

| C | CΔ7 | C6 | C | A7 |

T A B (¢) tablature

| D | D9 | D7 | D13 | G | G7 |

1.

| Gm7 | G7 | C | C°7 | Dm7 | G+ |

2.

| C | A♭7 | C |

Fine

| B♭9 | | A♭7 | |

| G9 | G+ | G6 | G7 |

D.C. al Fine

Finally, here's a heart-tugging ballad called "You've Changed." This is the chord progression from the sheet music in E♭. It's up to you to identify how each chord shape functions.

You've Changed

Eb△7   A°7   D+7   Bbm7   Bbm6

```
T|--0--------0-----------|
 |--8--------7-----6---6-|
A|--8----8----8--8---6---6*|
 |-------8*--8-----6---5-|
B|-------7---------------|
```

G⌀7   C7+   F9   B7   Bb7

```
T|-----------------------0-|
 |--6----5----4----4-----6-|
A|--6*---5----5*---4-------|
 |--5----5↑---5----4-----6-|
B|-------------------------|
```

1. Eb6   Cm7   Fm7   Bb7   2. Bbm7   Eb7

```
T|--0------------------------|
 |--8----8----1----1---•--6----6--|
A|--8----8----1----1------6----6*-|
 |--8----8----1----0---•--6----5--|
B|---------------------------|
```

Cm   Db△7   Bbm7   Eb7   Ab△7   Abm7

```
T|-------6------6------------------|
 |--8----6*-----6------8↑----------0-|
A|--8----5------6------8---0------1--|
 |--8-----------------8---1------1--|
B|-----------------------1---------|
```

Gm7   Eb△7   Eb7   Ab△7   Abm7

```
T|--0--------0---------------------|
 |--0--------0----6----5-----4-----|
A|--8--------------5----5*----4-----|
 |-----------8----4----4-----4-----|
B|---------------------------------|
```

E♭Δ7   G♭m6   Fm7   B♭7

```
T--0----------------------------------------
--8--------7------|--------------8----------
A----------7↑-----|-------10-----7----------
--8--------7------|-------10*----6----------
B-----------------|--------9------------------
```

When the inspiration strikes, try these progressions in different keys.

Some Useful Mini Chord Progressions

Here are some short chord combinations that can be used in most tunes. The first eight serve to connect a seventh chord with the major or seventh chord a fourth away (five frets higher or seven frets lower). The rhythm of the individual chords is not indicated, so it's up to you to tailor them to fit into a measure or two. You can use the tunes from the previous section as templates in which to fit these licks.

```
        C     CΔ7    C7    C7+   C13    F
T
A    8     8     8     9     10    10
     9     9*    8↑    9*    9     10
B   10     9     8     8     8     10
```

```
     C9   C11  C7#11 C9   C7#9   C7  C7b5   F
T    3    3
A    3*   3     7     7     8     8↑   9    10
B    2    3     7↑    8*    8     8    8    10
            7     8     8     8    7    10
```

In the previous example, you could start like this:

```
        C9
T
A     7
B     8*
      8
```

Then work to the left or right.

```
    C13  C7  C7b9     C7#9   C7b9  C11b9   F6
T                                          15
A   10   8   13   11   16   14  19   17    14*
    9    8↑  12   11↑  15   14  18   17↑   13
B   8    8   11   11   14   14  17   17
```

Note that for some passing chords, it is a moot point to try to identify them.

```
        C     C+    C6    C7     F
T                              8*
A     8     8↑   8↑↑        10
      9     9    9     9    10
B    10    10   10    10    10
```

39

C7   F7♭5   B♭7 E♭7♭5 A♭

```
T
A   15      14      13      12      13
    14      13      12      11      13
B   13      12      11      10      13
```

C7♭5♯9   F13 B♭7♭5♯9   E♭13   A♭

```
T  (16)    (15)    (14)    (13)    13
    16      15      14      13      13
A   15      14      13      12      13
    14      13      12      11      13
B
```

C   C+   CΔ13   C13   F6

```
T   5      5 †                     0
    5      5       9 †     10      10
A   5      5       9       9       10
                   9       8       10
B
```

C7   F

```
T   10     10      10      10      10
    11     10*     10†     10*†    10
A   12     11      10      9       10
B
```

Here is the famous Count Basie coda.

C   C+   C6

```
T                                  10
                                   9*
A   17              17             8
    17              17 †
B   17              17
```

Finally, here's a C minor chord with a descending bass line, identifiable in such standards as "My Funny Valentine," "Blue Skies," and "It Don't Mean a Thing if It Ain't Got That Swing."

Cm   CmΔ7   Cm7   Cm6

```
T
A   12       12        8        8
    13*      12 †      8        8*
B   13       12        8        7
```